Masterpieces of Russian Folk Art

Masterpieces of Russian Folk Art

I. Boguslavskaya **ZHOSTOVO**
Painted Trays

Interbook Moscow 1994

Compilation and preface by
I.Ya. Boguslavskaya

Consultation by	*A.F.*	*Yermoshkin*
	B.V.	*Grafov*
Translation by	*V.I.*	*Nemodruk*
Photography by	*V.P.*	*Belyi*
Design by	*L.L.*	*Likalter*

ISBN   5-7664-0994-8

The village of Zhostovo outside Moscow has become a symbol of unique folk art. For more than 150 years now many of its inhabitants have been developing the skill of decorating but one thing, trays. Their skillful hands have turned this household utensil into a work of art. Bouquets or garden and field flowers strewn against the black background adorn these trays, giving people joie-de-vivre and awakening admiration over the beauty and diversity of nature. Every human being shares these feelings, and therefore few people remain indifferent to the Zhostovo craft, which has long become world famous.

Zhostovo wares belong to the family of Russian lacquers, whose history goes back to the emergence of miniature lacquer painting on papier-mache in the village of Danilkovo near Fedoskino and the villages of Ostashkovo and Zhostovo, all in the Moscow Region, in the late 18th century. Lukutins' and Vishnyakovs' workshops were famous for their caskets, snuff boxes, purses, boxes, stamp cases, cigarette cases, tea boxes, match boxes, pencil stands, plates, folders and other small objects decorated with miniature paintings that offered free interpretations of popular scenes of easel painting and engraving. Started as lacquer miniature painting, the manufacture of trays gradually evolved into an independent craft, which engaged the inhabitants of several villages of the former Troitsk volost of the Moscow uyezd of the Moscow gubernia, such as Zhostovo, Ostashkovo, Khlebnikovo, Troitskoye, Sorokino, Novosiltsevo and Chivirevo. Zhostovo played the leading role and gave the name to the entire craft.

The first trays were made in Zhostovo in 1807, when Filipp Nikitich Vishnyakov* founded his workshop. After he moved to Moscow, his brother Taras carried on the family business. Yegor Vishnyakov started the manufacture of papier-mache and metal lacquers in the village of Ostashkovo 2km away from Zhostovo* in 1815, and Osip Filippovich Vishnyakov, whose name is associated with the flourishing of the craft, opened his workshop in 1825. Vishnyakovs' workshops were not the only ones operating in the area. During the same time Ivan Mitrofanovich Mitrofanov's workshop "remodelled trays" in Zhostovo. Andrei Alexeyevich Zaitsev started to produce trays in the village of Troitskoye in 1826. In the 1860s, Yegor Fyodorovich Belyayev, Timofei Maximovich Belyayev and Vassily Leontievich Leontiev opened their workshops in Zhostovo, Filipp Vassilyevich Shapkin and Yegor Sergeyev in the village of Sorokino, and Ivan Kolomensky and Nikita and Ivan Salov in the village of Khlebnikovo. Documents list twelve workshops* operating in the 1840s and the early 1850s. The manufacture of trays, now made not only of papier-mache but also of iron, emerged as a fairly developed craft in the Moscow region by that time.

Every tray was usually handled by three craftsmen - a smith, who produced shapes, a spatler, who covered the tray with a layer of ground, and a painter, who did the painting. After the tray was dried, the ground-worker covered it with lacquer. In the beginning the workshop master and members of his family worked on a par with other employees. With the expansion of business there appeared hired laborers, and the master increasingly turned into an entrepreneur who did not always have an intimate knowledge of production. In the 1870s through the 1880s tray making involved more than 240 workers in the Moscow region. Osip Vishnyakov's and Yegor Belyayev's workshops were the largest in Zhostovo and employed respectively 59 and 51 craftsmen*. The earliest Zhostovo trays surviving in museum collections date to that period. Their dating and provenance primarily from the Vishnyakovs' workshops is certified by trademarks on the reverse side of trays, which give the name of the factory owner and the list of prizes won at major art and industry exhibitions, as well as handicrafts shows.

As the Zhostovo craftsmen expanded production, they took account of

The Index of the Third Moscow Exhibition of Russian Manufacturers of 1843, Moscow, 1843, p. 314. *

Moscow Gubernia Crafts. Collection of Statistics for the Moscow Gubernia, Moscow, 1882, Vol. 7, Iss. 3, pp. 335-351. *

Isayev A. A., Moscow Gubernia Crafts, Moscow, 1876, Part 2 (Tables to Ch. 1 "Metalworking Crafts"). Krapivina, I. A., From Zhostovo Craft History (19th - early 20th cent.). Russian Cities (Study and Documents), Iss. 5, Moscow, 1982, pp. 76-77. *

Isayev A. A., Op. cit., Tables. *

and absorbed the experience of other tray-makers. They were prompted the idea of replacing papier-mache with metal, which was hardier, by trays from Nizhny Tagil, which had become a well-known production center way back in the 17th century. Those masters were making large trays painted from original canvasses or engravings. In the mid-19th century they were supplanted by more common-place trays of diverse shapes; they were adorned with foliate ornaments, which were characteristic of many folk utensils produced in the Urals. Nizhny Tagil remained Russia's leading tray-maker till the 1870s-1880s, when the Zhostovo products began strongly to compete with them.

In the mid-19th century, the St. Petersburg tray-making industry became quite famous. Their specialty was trays of sophisticated shapes and designs, painted with flowers, fruit, birds amongst shells and intricate curls. Many Zhostovo smiths and painters used to go to St. Petersburg to work or to sell their wares.

The tray as a household utensil had been known since times immemorial, but in the 19th century the demand for trays rose as a result of the growth of cities and the expansion of the network of hotels, eateries and bars, where trays were used both for their immediate purpose and as interior decorations. It was that new market that enabled the Zhostovo masters to establish themselves as a distinctive tray-making industry. They took into account the experience of other production centers, but instead of merely borrowing the shapes and techniques they liked, they reworked them into their own inimitable style. They borrowed many shapes - including the guitar-like, round, octagonal and rectangular ones - from Nizhny Tagil. However, the Zhostovo smiths improved and diversified them by varying sizes and proportions, introducing smooth curves to join the plate of the tray to its border, and adorning the carved handles with intricate designs.

The Zhostovo masters admired the virtuoso mastery of St. Petersburg trays and learned from them the art of decorative still life, also adapting it to fit their own wares. Along with absorbing some of the techniques of other tray-makers, the Zhostovo craftsmen primarily tried to develop their own, local traditions. Zhostovo tray-making was born of the miniature lacquer painting craft that was practised in villages and townships around Moscow, and that umbilical cord was not cut for a long time. Until the 20th century the trays and lacquered wares were produced in the same workshop and painted by the same masters. Even after tray-making had spun off as a distinctive industry, the Zhostovo tray painters continued to improve the techniques of processing lacquered papier-mache boxes while using the same grounds, lacquers and oil paints. The specific Fedos-kino techniques of multilayer painting, subsequent light brushes against metal-lized or multicolored backgrounds and mother-of-pearl inlay were borrowed from lacquer miniature painting and applied to tray-making.

The scenes painted on early trays - troika carriages, tea-parties and rus-tic character scenes - were close to the compositions used on lacquer miniatures. Engravings from fashionable canvases by Russian, Ukrainian and European mas-ters that were reprinted extensively by many magazines were copied on a large scale: they were adapted and modified to fit the decorative nature of tray paining. Compositions were simplified and skilfully integrated into the diverse shapes and sizes of trays, and artists used the laws of perspective to create the impression of depth and volume and balance parts of the composition and colors to give cadence to their works.

One early example of this style is a 1980s tray from the workshop of O. F. Vishnyakov, which shows a "summer troika." A cart drawn by three horses is spotlighted, as it were, in the center of an oval tray. There are two girls and a driver lad in the cart. The postures of the horses and people bespeak fast move-ment. The shrubs and trees standing out barely from the dark indicate the scenery. The bright colors of the people's dresses complement the decorative composition of the painting. A Ukrainian genre scene on another tray from O. Vishnyakov's workshop and especially a popular scene of a "tea-party" on a tray from V. O. Vishnyakov's workshop were done in a similar style.

A tray showing Peter the Great on Lake Ladoga appears to hail back to the origins of the Zhostovo industry. The F. T. B. brand on the reverse indicates that the tray must have been made from Timofey Belyayev's workshop, which was producing in Zhostovo in the mid-19th century. The painter used a lithograph* from the 1812 engraving "Peter the Great Caught in a Storm on Lake Ladoga" by the French artist C. Steiben, which was quite popular in Russia in the 19th cen-tury and which was reprinted by various magazines. Nizhny Tagil masters faith-fully reproduced it on their trays*, but the Zhostovo painters only used the idea, but modified the figures of the characters and their postures in the composition. The romantic elan of the painting was enhanced by the expressions on the faces of the characters and by the stormy clouds and bolts of lighting in the skies. The decorative colors of the characters' dresses are harmonized with the easel-paint-ing character of the scene, which looks like a framed canvas; the frame is simu-lated by a broad ornamental border, which extends from the intricate sides of the

The Russian Museum. Russian *
Folk Art of the 17th to the
20th Century, Exhibition
Catalogue. New Acquisitions
(1977-1987), Leningrad,
1988, p. 44.

Krapiwina I., Russishe *
handbemalte Tabletts,
Leningrad, 1981, S. 5-6.

tray onto the main field. It shows a succession of oval leaves painted on Dutch gold, which are characteristic of the Zhostovo style, and spiral-like curves.

Alongside using genre scenes, Zhostovo craftsmen increasingly developed their own style of decorative floral compositions, which became dominant by the mid-1880s. Trays of that period are characterized by a pronouncedly original style which evolved in the preceding decades. Local artistic traditions and the creative development of the main accomplishments of other crafts enabled Zhostovo craftsmen to evolve their original style and an unique system of the local craft that are manifest in every piece dating to that period.

In one of the trays from O.F. Vishnyakov's workshop decorated with a bouquet against a white background the oval plane gently flows into a sharply bent border. The shape is well-proportioned, resilient and elegant. A bunch of roses, bindweeds and dahlias entwined with leaves and grasses, typical of trays of that period, is in the center. Though representations were flat, the exquisite curves of plants and their characteristic interpretations created a three-dimensional impression. The natural placement of flowers went well with the balanced parts of the bouquet and the rhythmic alternation of similar motifs and colorful spots. The conventional airiness of the background was attained with the help of light shadows. The soft shades were in perfect harmony with the ivory background. The composition was held together by a golden ornament of vine leaves and grapes gently flowing from the edge of the tray onto its central part. Such borders were called "uborka" (adornment) in Zhostovo.

A tight bunch of roses, camomiles, columbines and other small flowers and leaves, which looked quite authentic even though their nature remained unspecified, was painted against a black background on another tray attributed to V.T. Belyayev's workshop and dated to the late 19th - early 20th centuries. The shape was formed with the help of energetic brushwork and white highlights, with its conventionality enhanced by thin stems and light loop-like curls of tendrils. The shape of the bouquet with overhanging sides echoes the shape of the oval and slightly curving tray. The rows of ornamental strips along the edge look like a rich frame of a peculiar floral still life.

The indispensable elements of gradual Zhostovo painting, which form a certain system, a professional artistic canon to this day characteristic of the Zhostovo craft, can be traced in these items.

Zhostovo painting started with "zamalyovka," in which the silhouettes of flowers and leaves, organized into a bouquet composition in the painter's imagination, were sketched in whitened paint. After the initial painting dried, shadows were laid in scumbling (transparent) colors. This shadowing technique immersed the bouquet deep into the background, outlining the shadowy parts of plants. Next came the most important stage of "prokladka" - the thick painting of the main body. The bouquet took shape through minute details and highlights, giving birth to either a contrasting or harmonized composition color scheme. "Blikovka," or highlighting emphasized volume and lighting, finalizing the shape and making it conventionally material. The subsequent "chertyozhka" picked out the details in swift and light outlines of petals and leaves, the veins and seeds in the flower cups. The painting is finished off with "privyazka," the tying up of the bouquet with the background with the help of thin grasses and tendrils.

The consequent techniques of Zhostovo painting formed, as it were, the ABC of the solid local craft. It did not prevent craftsmen from free improvization, the selective interpretation of every element and the subordination of the entire system to the author's unique personal style. That system remained unchanged in the various trends of Zhostovo painting that became manifest in the works of the 1880s through the 1900s.

One such trend was associated with gorgeous expensive trays decorated with bunches of flowers reminiscent of floral still life, and another trend with modest common wares painted in the tradition of folk ornament. The former trend is richly illustrated by many trays reproduced in the present publication, whereas the latter is exemplified by a small tray from the Vishnyakov Brothers' workshop. Its guitar shape, bright orange background and central composition make it similar to Nizhny Tagil wares. However, the nature of flowers and rounded three-dimensional fruit, and inherent rhythm which attuned them to the shape of the tray, as well as the presence of all elements of Zhostovo painting testify that it was done by an anonymous Zhostovo master craftsman.

In broadening the expressive means of their craft, Zhostovo painters were devising new techniques of ornamental painting. They came up with the "smoking" technique, for example, which enabled them to paint the tray with a vibrant ornament resembling the tortoise shell design, locally known as "pod chervyachok" (which roughly translates as "worm-like"). A similar technique was used in papier-mache lacquers, but it was originally adapted to tray-painting and employed either as an independent ornamental design, or as "uborka," the final embellishment, or in combination with rich gilded bordering in order to make the decorative background even more ornate.

The Zhostovo masters painted their trays on colored and golden backgrounds as well as on black and white ones. The surface of the tray was prepared with bronze or aluminum dust which, showing through lacquer, shone like gold and resembled the famous Khokhloma wares. The colors looked especially vibrant against the golden background and the tray seemed a really precious item.

In the olden times no one kept any record of the masters' names. Only one name of Osip Yefimovich Burbyshev (1867-1919) of the old Vishnyakovs' workshops came down to us. The tales of the remarkable gift of that master, who worked for M. P. Vishnyakov in Ostashkovo in the late 19th and early 20th centuries, are still alive in Zhostovo. He could fill any order, however challenging. Indeed, several of the surviving trays done by him stand out for their artistry and virtuoso mastery of the local artistic skills. A bunch of flowers with two roses in the heart of it spreads freely against the shimmering golden background of a small intricately shaped tray. The stalks of the flowers are intricately bent in natural movement, organically filling in the background and keeping the composition in balance. The shapes of the flowers are fairly realistic, although painted in the conventional Zhostovo manner. The sense of depth is conveyed with rhythmic energetic strokes of the brush. The fine blades of grass create the impression of an airy background, against which bright colors stand out.

Burbyshev's work was an outstanding contribution that enthroned the decorative bunch of flowers as the leading trend in 20th century Zhostovo craft.

In the 1910s, Zhostovo tray-making, like many other folk crafts, was hit by a crisis. The demand for trays had slumped, and production was shrinking. Painters and smiths were leaving their workshops for farming or seasonal work. The die-hards started an artel in the Novosiltsevo village in 1912, but it shortly folded up.

It was only in the 1920s, with the overall revival of folk crafts and the rebirth of artels across the country, that they re-emerged around Zhostovo; in 1928 they merged into the Metallopodnos artel, which in 1960 took its present name of the Zhostovo decorative painting factory.

Zhostovo fell on hard times in the 1920s and 1930s. The tendency for the uncompromising assertion of modernity and realism that were common for Soviet art prompted the authorities in charge of the folk crafts to try to influence their traditional developmental trends and impose on the Zhostovo painters easel-painting and naturalist models of ornamental and thematic compositions that had been devised by professional artists without any regard for the specific *features of the local craft. The leading Zhostovo painters understood that those innovations were alien to the very nature of folk art, so they effectively countered those new trends and infused new ideas into the traditional school of painting.*

Much credit for the preservation and development of the best traditions of the local craft goes to the classic Zhostovo masters of the period, among them I. S. Leontiev, P. S. Kurzin, D. S. Kledov and A. I. Leznov. Each of them made a contribution to the art of painting by embroidering on the Zhostovo techniques and enriching their collective fabric with their individual creative quests and accomplishments.

In asserting the local tradition, painters occasionally produced ingenuous copies of old trays from the Vishnyakovs' workshops of the early 20th century. One example is P. S. Kurzin's tray "Tobacco Leaves." The hallmarks of the painter's original compositions are simplicity of design and virtuoso techniques. One of his trays is a still life: a vase with a bunch of flowers stands on a table, the wood texture of its boards pointedly highlighted. It stands out against the "tortoise-shell" background. The composition, edged by several ornamental borders, looks like a framed canvas. The painting effectively makes the tray a work of art, reducing its utilitarian purpose to insignificance. This, like the choice of still life as such, is Kurzin's bow to easel-painting, which was the fad at the time, but the entire composition followed the laws of Zhostovo decorative painting. The flowers have depth, but do not look over-naturalistic, and the still life is dominated by strict rhythm in the placement of groups of flowers, spots of color and shades of light and dark. Though the composition is static, is details, painted with ease and gusto, look dynamic.

The vertically positioned bunch of flowers on another tray also looks pointedly picturesque, but the decorative theme is all-pervasive as well: the bunch stands out against the black background, the details are finely drawn up to give complexity to the picture, and the sophisticated interplay of shades and colors is governed by a certain rhythm.

K. V. Gribkov's works also bear the imprint of still life easel-painting. The artist, trained as a decorator, painted trays from drafts rather than improvised, as the Zhostovo masters traditionally did. However, he adapted his professional skills to the conventional local techniques. his manner is characterized by the dimensional presentation of flowers and leaves, the intricate ornamental drawing of their shapes, soft and harmonious colors and subdued decorative embroidery. His hallmark was the crowns of the flowers painted with thick circular highlights, which made them look highly ornamental.

I. S. Leontiev, the leading Zhostovo painter till 1945, based many of his accomplishments on peasant ornaments. His bunches of flowers perfectly fitted the shapes of the trays. The drawings were severe and academic, and the finely executed details were complemented by rich highlights that made the flowers stand out from the background. The plants seem to be bathing in air. Although easily recognizable, they are not naturalistic. The impression of relative perspective is balanced by the flat background, which had a special part to play in Leontiev's trays. He greatly enriched the use of colored, golden and silver backgrounds in the Zhostovo tradition. The bright colors play even more riotously against such backgrounds. Leontiev's works stand out for their fine technique and sophisticated color scheme.

Brothers D. S. and N. S. Kledovs followed different trends of the Zhostovo painting. D. S. Kledov was a true master of composition endowed with an expressive style. Flowers and fruit in his still lifes are compact and seem to be bathing in air. He strictly adhered to the consecutive methods of Zhostovo painting, bringing them to a high level of perfection.

N. S. Kledov occupied a special place in Zhostovo craft. His works exemplified the so called primitive or naive painting. Fancy landscapes with small houses tinged by scarlet sunsets, flying flocks of birds and couples boating on ponds with reflections on the water surface adorn his trays. Space is organized with the help of curtains and divided into three planes. Local colors were used in combination with the graphic treatment of details, which made his landscape paintings exuberant and decorative. Akin to tawdry rugs and signboards, they mirrored townsfolk dreams of a better life.

A. I. Leznov's trays had the qualities of a decorative panel. Big in size and often round in shape, his trays were reminiscent of easel still lifes. Leznov worked with professional artists who designed models for tray painting. The incompatibility of the principles of easel painting with those of decorative Zhostovo still lifes posed great difficulties, which Leznov managed to surmount after a while, preserving the traditional Zhostovo style intact and enriching it with the experience of easel painting. Emulating the still life model, he often painted bouquets and fruit in vases and baskets, attuning them to the shape of the tray and accentuating that shape. Central compositions are well balanced and lit on all sides, with the colors enhanced by the black background. Leznov used boldly and flexibly all the expressive means of Zhostovo painting, interchanging them in every particular piece of work executed now in contrasting colors, now in the fine gradation of shades. He made a virtuoso use of highlights, tracing volumes and shapes of flowers and leaves with visible brush strokes. His craftsmanship was diverse and very artistic.

The development of Zhostovo craft was interrupted by the Great Patriotic War of 1941-1945, after which followed a no less difficult stage of its history. The specific nature of decorative and applied arts was ignored, easel elements, genre scenes, naturalism and the bathos of sumptuous ceremonious style contaminated handicrafts of that period, including the works of Zhostovo craftsmen. Fewer trays were painted, while the output of toy buckets and spades increased; models and stencils were commonly employed. Despite these unfavorable circumstances, local craftsmen carried on their family businesses and preserved the age-old traditions of the craft, enriching it with their creative experience and handing it over to the younger generation.

A. P. Gogin, who was the leader and chief artist of Zhostovo craft from 1948 to 1961, played an outstanding role in Zhostovo history. He spent his long life in his native village, studying at its old workshops, organizing there an artel in the 1920s, producing a host of diverse works and teaching the traditional craft to numerous apprentices.

As an artist Gogin matured under the guidance of I. S. Leontiev, whose works he admired. He also studied attentively the works of his fellow craftsmen Leznov and Kurzin, as well as old St Petersburg trays. All that left an imprint in his memory and helped him develop his own style. Gogin had a preference for color, white and golden backgrounds and mother-of-pearl inlays. Every background called for a certain color scheme, composition and design. The master created various shapes - round, winged, figured and oval, and employed different composition patterns, such as strewn or tight bouquets. His favorite flowers were roses, poppies and tulips, to which he added conventional, albeit no less authentic, flowers. Gogin's roses can always be recognized by their hanging deep many-petalled cups, half-open and elongated sideways. He had a lyrical bent and glorified Nature's harmony in his flowers.

M. R. Mitrofanov was endowed with an original gift. His works are close to folk ornaments. His bouquets or wreaths of flowers have a special ornamental rhythm or are presented as ornamental compositions. Exquisitely drawn simple shapes look flattened and spread out, their details graphically worked out. Bright local colors create a cheerful palette, enhanced with a frame of golden wreaths.

The master often painted on Dutch gold and placed highlights against the golden background. Mitrofanov's trays are sumptuous and ornamental, manifesting the folk nature of his works.

In 1940, the Fedoskino vocational school opened a department of Zhostovo painting to train young craftsmen. Two remarkable Zhostovo painters, P. I. Plakhov and V. I. Dyuzhayev, taught there for many years, the activity that was responsible for their emergence as original masters. They trained several generations of young craftsmen, who developed in their own way the Zhostovo painting traditions, and themselves represented two different, highly dissimilar aspects of the local craft.

P. I. Plakhov studied under I. S. Leontiev and A. I. Leznov and carried on A. P. Gogin's lyrical trend. The experience of his teachers and his being an erudite in the history of European tray painting helped Plakhov evolve his own inimitable style, in which perfect craftsmanship combined with a poetic and lyrical spirit. Plakhov had a superb command of all local painting techniques and employed them with great skill. His bouquets with elegantly drawn flowers and delicately curving stems glow and shine against the black background which acquires a velvet-like depth. The master made a novel use of his rich palette in every new tray, seeking to arrive at a tonal color scheme.

V. I. Dyuzhayev frequently arranged his compositions relying on contrasts, now placing deliberately cold bluish-white roses against a glaring orange-red background, now alternating well-lit and darkened flowers and clusters of rowan-berries executed in warm brownish-purple shades. Outwardly tranquil and balanced, Dyuzhayev's works are imbued with inward intensity. His poignant coloring and at times inordinately intense hues occasionally ooze anxiety, still enhanced by the postures of frightened birds sitting on the flowers, looking warily askance and ready to take off at any moment. Dynamic and imaginative painting made Dyuzhayev's tray gorgeously decorative, strictly conforming to the Zhostovo canons and with the composition fully attuned to the well thought-out shape of the tray. At the same time there is a certain emotional spontaneity about his works.

Another stage in the history of Zhostovo craft started in the 1960s and continues to our day. Overcoming tendencies leaning toward easel painting and naturalism, tray painting has been gaining in prestige and popularity not only owing to large-scale output of serial works, but also owing to unique items that increasingly attracted public attention at numerous exhibitions both at home and abroad.

A young generation of painters trained by Gogin, Plakhov and Dyuzhayev joined Zhostovo workshops in the 1950s. Today they are the local leaders, who in their turn are training their successors. Zhostovo craft has progressed in the past thirty years and became enriched by remarkable works of art and gifted artisans, who elevated the traditions of a local craft to the level of unique folk art.

*Ever since its outset Zhostovo craft has been developed by several generations of craftsmen, who formed painter dynasties. It is being carried on today by the familial Belyayev, Kledov, Antipov, Saveliev, Gogin and Vishnyakov clans. A group of leading Zhostovo painters was awarded the Repin State Prize of the Russian Federation in 1977. Many of them have been granted the honorable title of the Merited Artist of Russia, are members of the Artists' Union, have been decorated with medals of the Academy of Arts, and have won diplomas and awards at numerous exhibitions of different levels. Their works are stored as a national treasury and exhibited by major national museums. Constantly perfecting their craftsmanship, Zhostovo painters give free rein to improvization, demonstrating diverse styles and techniques. B. V. Grafov, a remarkable painter in his own right and Zhostovo's permanent artistic director and chief artist since 1961, gives the following graphic description: "The factory employs over 200 artists. They are all true master craftsmen. Every one of them is a personality with his or her own view of the world. They all work in comparatively equal conditions, using the same tray shapes, materials, brushes and paints. But by the end of the workday I always marvel at the very different results they achieve. As a matter of fact, they are very different, though working in the same conditions; they employ successions of the same techniques, but interpret them differently; they use the same paints, but they mix them on the palette in different combinations; and their brushwork styles are so different... . I am always amazed by the fanciful play of imagination of all masters and find in their works a source of inspiration for my own work. Just look at this painting and you'll feel pleasure not less than you do from music!" ***

Koromyslov B. I., "Boris *
Grafov." Soviet Decorative Art,
Iss. 7, Moscow, 1983, p. 111.

Modern Zhostovo craftsmen are increasingly turning the tray from a household object into a work of art, and decorative Zhostovo painting is elevated to the level of an independent genre capable of addressing directly people's thoughts and feelings. B. Grafov goes on to say: "Zhostovo trays are increasingly acquiring the meaning of decorative objects rather than a mere household utensil by virtue of the special importance of their painting. Our trays are both beautiful and meaningful. At first sight the painting seems to be finishing off and adorning the tray, but there is more to it than meets the eye... Take a closer look and you'll be enchanted with the meaning of the bouquet... . Every flower is looking at you and telling you something, or reminding you of something. These flowers are inimitable and always different, each with its own original character, and even the artist himself will not be able to produce the same bouquet."*

Zhostovo craftsmen often paint panel-like trays, which have a certain emotional, symbolic meaning expressed at times in the work's expressive name. In any interior a modern tray or panel is an emotional meaningful center radiating the sense of beauty and joy of life.

The outstanding artist N. P. Antipov of a family of Zhostovo craftsmen called one of his trays "Rus." Its general symbolic meaning lies not merely in the choice of typical flowers for the bouquet. The author interprets it in a broader sense of movement, the generosity of the land and the richness of nature as symbolized by flowers. This idea is consistently expressed in the intricate shape of the tray, repeated in the curving stalks of bindweeds and white, sharp-petalled daffodils and also in the dynamic wreath and border in contrast to the outwardly static but full of inherent intensity bouquet in the center, with its likewise intense design of flowers and their powerful color scheme.

Antipov is an artist who is well-versed in the secrets of the local craft. Nothing is too difficult for him. His every work has an integral artistic meaning. Even his choice of flowers is connected with the shape and type of the tray he paints. His trays differ in size, shape, composition and background color; he often employs mother-of-pearl inlays, making the tray even more decorative with transparent highlights and enriching the coloring with fine nuances. As the artist puts it, "high mastery is attained not all of a sudden, but slowly, with great difficulty and through enormous practice."* Both his trays and those produced by many Zhostovo masters prove his point.

As distinct from Antipov's expressive temperament, N. N. Goncharova has a lyrical bend, apparently inherited from her teacher A. P. Gogin. Her trays are characteristically called "Tenderness," "Joy," "Charming," "Resplendent" and "Festive." According to the artist, "every Zhostovo craftsman has his or her favorite flowers. For me they are roses, poppies and Aquilegia. I love roses most of all. They easily lend themselves to fantasy and can be interpreted differently."* Roses form diverse compositions in her trays, which have both simple and ornate shapes, now brought together in a centrally-placed bouquet, now framing the figured edge, now forming wreaths or strewn about the entire background, acquiring a different expressive meaning and creating an impression of exultant festiv-

* Koromyslov B. I., "Boris Grafov." Soviet Decorative Art, Iss. 7, Moscow, 1983, p. 107

* Modern Zhostovo Craft. Painters Speak About Their Work. Folk Art. Traditions and Quests. Collected Papers of the Handicrafts Research Institute, Iss. 9, Moscow, 1979, p. 51.

* Ibid., p. 50.

ity, tender thoughts or quiet contemplation. Depending on what she has in mind, the artist uses contrasting transparent colors on a mother-of-pearl foundation against the velvety black background or else delicately harmonized shades against color, golden or complex-palette backgrounds. Every one of Goncharova's works evokes admirations by the immaculate realization of the idea, the fine lyrical content and exquisitely beautiful painting.

Y. P. Lapshin develops the poetic trend of his teacher P. I. Plakhov. There are also a lot of roses and peonies in his bouquets, whose rich fluffy petals seem to be always bathing in the air. The background also serves as an airy medium of sorts. Sometimes the master places bouquets asymmetrically, as it were, "from the corner." Nevertheless, parts are always well-balanced in his compositions, forming a proportionate relationship with the background, while the bouquets are characterized by a delicate palette rich in hues. Lapshin offers an interesting explanation of the peculiarities of Zhostovo painting: "Many may find it strange that we do not paint live flowers, say, a natural rose. Our rose is something different from flowers on rose bushes. It will no longer seem strange, however, if you take our brush in your hand. Our brush paints in circular, soft and delicate strokes. It hates sharp angles and direct lines... . The Zhostovo bouquet is a community of flowers, different in shape and similar in spirit. In large measure they are true to life and largely conventional at the same time. Even the color of Zhostovo roses - white, yellow, blue (at times even dark blue), pink and red - is conventional.

"Our flowers are not a rigid scheme. They live their own inner life, and they change all the time. We observe nature, go to the museum and look at postcards and books. The flowers we see involuntarily become engraved in our memory and then in some way influence the look of our bouquets."*

B. V. Grafov can be called an experimenter artist. His good knowledge of history and the artistic heritage of the local craft facilitate his creative quests. Consciously drawing on the different trends and techniques of Zhostovo painting, he copes with a concrete artistic task in every particular piece of work. In some cases it is the elaboration of a flat ornamental composition employing the technique of fast folk motif painting, in others adherence to the traditions of a classically strict bouquet still life executed in a tonal color scheme, and in still others it is a decorative panel reflecting a certain state of nature in bouquets. Thus, the "Moscow Morning" conveys the delicate charm of roses and branches of a blossoming apple-tree with the halo of green leaves. Lit by the pale reflection of the

Modern Zhostovo Craft. *
Painters Speak About Their
Work. Folk Art. Traditions
and Quests. Collected
Papers of the Handicrafts
Research Institute, Iss. 9,
Moscow, 1979,
p. 46-47

dawn and as if washed in dew, they set out in relief from the depth of the black background, evoking a mental picture of a morning landscape. On the "Bouquet. Morning" tray roses and irises with delicate light petals are set against the cold shimmering blue background, creating an image of a frosty morning.

Grafov works with different shapes of trays and other household objects, be it saucers or bread-trays that craftsmen used to paint in the past. He often experiments with metallic color backgrounds, employing Dutch gold and mother-of-pearl inlays. His skills seem boundless. One of his latest works, "Twin Dandelions" decorative tray, impresses not so much by the correspondence of its content to its name as by its masterful technique of execution and superb artistic craftsmanship.

N. N. Mazhayev displays the diversity of his creative endeavors. His earlier works were characterized by the desire to copy as close as possible the beauty and charm of simple field and garden flowers. With the passage of time his compositions and flower designs grew more intricate and his bouquets acquired profound imagery and at times symbolic meaning. Some works give a lyrical reflection of the natural harmony of flowers, others look austere and laconic in oversimplified ornamental compositions prompted by folk paintings and printed cloths. Mazhayev belongs to the few Zhostovo craftsmen who sought a modern rendition of genre compositions drawing on the traditions of popular prints, posters and old genre scenes used on Zhostovo trays. In one of his recent works, "Moscow Environs," Mazhayev gives a generalized picture of local nature reminiscent of N. P. Antipov's "Rus." There is a bouquet of camomiles, globeflowers and bluebells against a shimmering bright green background. The unusual shape of the figured horizontally elongated oval tray enhanced by ornate framing produces the impression of a conventional space locked within the tray surface and capable of giving an idea of the whole by its part in keeping with folk art traditions. The sight of this work brings to mind sunlit flourishing fields of the Moscow region, even though the picture was made in keeping with the conventional canons of Zhostovo painting rather than being painted from nature.

M. P. Savelyev also has his own style and forms of bouquets made now of uniform flowers, now of different ones. His trays are often round, their names - "Horizon," "Elegy" or "Rain" - breeding associations. The as it were vibrating representation of thin branches, drooping with raindrops, placed rhythmically along the upper edge and sides of the tray, produces the physical impression of rain. Savelyev paints against black and color backgrounds, which play an active part in the overall color scheme, and makes a skillful use of metallized foundations, Dutch gold and diverse ornamental framing. His "Elegy" decorative tray stands out for its delicate palette and lyrical mood.

V. V. Kledov, another artist who comes from a family of Zhostovo crafsmen, works in a more traditional vein. He adheres to the behests of old Zhostovo masters, the patriarchs of local art of the 1930s through the 1950s, as far as the bouquet composition and the sequence of local techniques are concerned. His bouquets are deliberately detailed and colorful, at times to the extent of being overcrowded with a variety of hues, and yet conveying the feeling of joy and plenitude of life. One of his best works - the "Ornamental" tray - shows a thick bouquet in the center, with paired garlands at the corners forming, as it were, a whole wreath. The near-natural shapes of his flowers are softened by the measured rhythm of color spots and the exquisite floral design. The entire composition is skillfully enclosed in the soft guitar-shaped tray.

V. V. Kledov, N. N. Mazhayev and M. P. Savelyev have recently started to paint fruit on trays. This tradition existed among old Zhostovo masters but was rarely carried on since the 1930s. Every artist interprets in his own way the measure of conventionality and naturalness in painting fruit and berries.

V. N. Pyzhov treats every tray as a veritable work of art. An innovative version is there to be found unexpectedly in each of his works. He personally forges his tray forms, guided by the experience of old Zhostovo and St Petersburg masters and often uses intricate shapes, including the rare "shell" shape borrowed from the Rococo style. Pyzhov's flowers and bouquets, always enclosed in richly ornamented bordering, are distinguished by fine execution and often have a gala air about them. Characteristically enough, the artist is fond of using gold and silver paints and Dutch gold as a foundation. The "Autumn Flowers" tray is typical in this respect, with its bouquet placed from the corner and masterfully developed golden color scheme.

Many a unique work of art was produced by other well-known Zhostovo painters, such as L. N. Vishnyakov (a direct descendant of one of the founders of the craft), N. I. Gogin, V. I. Letkov, V. V. Zhmylev, N. D. and G. P. Belyayevs, Z. A. Kledova, R. A. Vishnyakova and N. A. Pichugina.

In the period from the 1970s to the 1980s young painters took up the craft and showed their worth at numerous exhibitions. Among them were N. N. Antipov, A. N. Mazhayev, L. Y. Dyatlova, M. E. Domnikova, S. S. Gogin, S. A. Filippov, O. A. Gavrilov and V. V. Rizin. Some of them carry on their family businesses, adding new ideas to tray and decorative panel painting and developing in their own way different trends of Zhostovo painting.

For example, T. Sholokhova and M. Antipova pay tribute to the beauty of old St Petersburg trays and offer their variations of the theme.

N. N. Antipov often employs the smoking technique. The "wormlike" design in the "Galactic" tray uniformly fills the unusual elliptic shape with alternating sharp and rounded wings and creates an image of measured rhythmic movement with its curves. The smoking technique is used in the decorative "Jubilee" tray in the middle of a broad ornate border spreading from the wings of the tray onto the central part. The image hinges on the contrast between the dark framing and the lightly painted bouquet of bindweeds, camomiles, pansies and the indispensable many-petalled rose in the center against the golden background. Highlighted by confident strokes, the flowers and leaves look moderately three-dimensional.

L. Y. Dyatlova demonstrates in her works the same lyrical talent as is characteristic of her mother, N. N. Goncharova. The "September" tray, in which the author was attracted by faded, tender shades rather than bright autumn colors, is indicative in this respect. Tea-roses, enhanced by tiny blue flowers, are placed against the warm brown background. The soft rounded design of petals and leaves echoes the small oval shape of the tray in keeping with its intimate nature. Her "Bouquet Against a White Background" has an exquisitely cool color scheme.

A. N. Mazhayev's tray "Camomiles" is original both in its guitar-like shape with figured wings and its unusual composition, in which two balanced groups of flowers fill the central part.

S. A. Filippov has a predilection for ornate trays with richly ornamented framing, gold painting on a Dutch gold foundation. M. E. Domnikova paints a decorative still life in her "Earth's Gravitation" tray. A big spreading bouquet with large peonies in the center extends nearly throughout the entire surface. The light from the center fades out toward the edges, where the leaves and flowers disappear in the profoundly black background. Metallized foundations in the leaves produce a play of colors and luminescence. The small plants in the wreath on V. V. Rizin's tray disappear in the same way in the dark-blue background. Reddish reflections from the middle of the three-tiered border create highlights, ensuring the decorative effect.

Other young painters make their contributions to the general cause. Working side by side and on a par with recognized masters, they are looking for their own original trends in the local craft.

Zhostovo trays have transformed from a household object into full-fledged decorative panels in the course of their history, and the craft which served as an auxiliary source of income for farmers, has acquired the status of a unique Russian folk art.

Decorative Zhostovo painting is on the rise today. This is not to say, however, that craftsmen experience no difficulties or problems. The latter are encountered in all spheres of our culture which has to withstand unbridled latterday commercialization. Imitators seek to copy the Zhostovo style and even the individual manner of Zhostovo painters. Only ignorant people, however, can be thus deluded. Local craftsmen have top professionalism attained in painstaking yearlong creative quests, perfection of craftsmanship and constant emulation of the best specimens of the old masters' legacy. Mention should also be made of the study of the history of art, classical still lifes and various types of Russian applied and folk art, which nourish the creative potential of local painters. Given exacting selection and assimilation in keeping with the local canons, all that offers wide opportunities to improve and develop tray painting. "We cannot see tradition as an aim in itself and mark time," says B. V. Grafov. "We must forcefully develop the historical craft, enriching it with new shapes and new content."* Leading Zhostovo craftsmen are well aware of that. Their loyalty to their craft and devotion to their creative work are a source of inspiration for young craftsmen, which ensures that craftsmanship is handed down to younger generations and hence opens prospects for the further progress of the craft.

* Modern Zhostovo Craft. Painters Speak About Their Work. Folk Art. Traditions and Quests. Collected Papers of the Handicrafts Research Institute, Iss. 9, Moscow, 1979, p. 40.

Illustrations

N.N. Antipov
"JUBILEE"

1

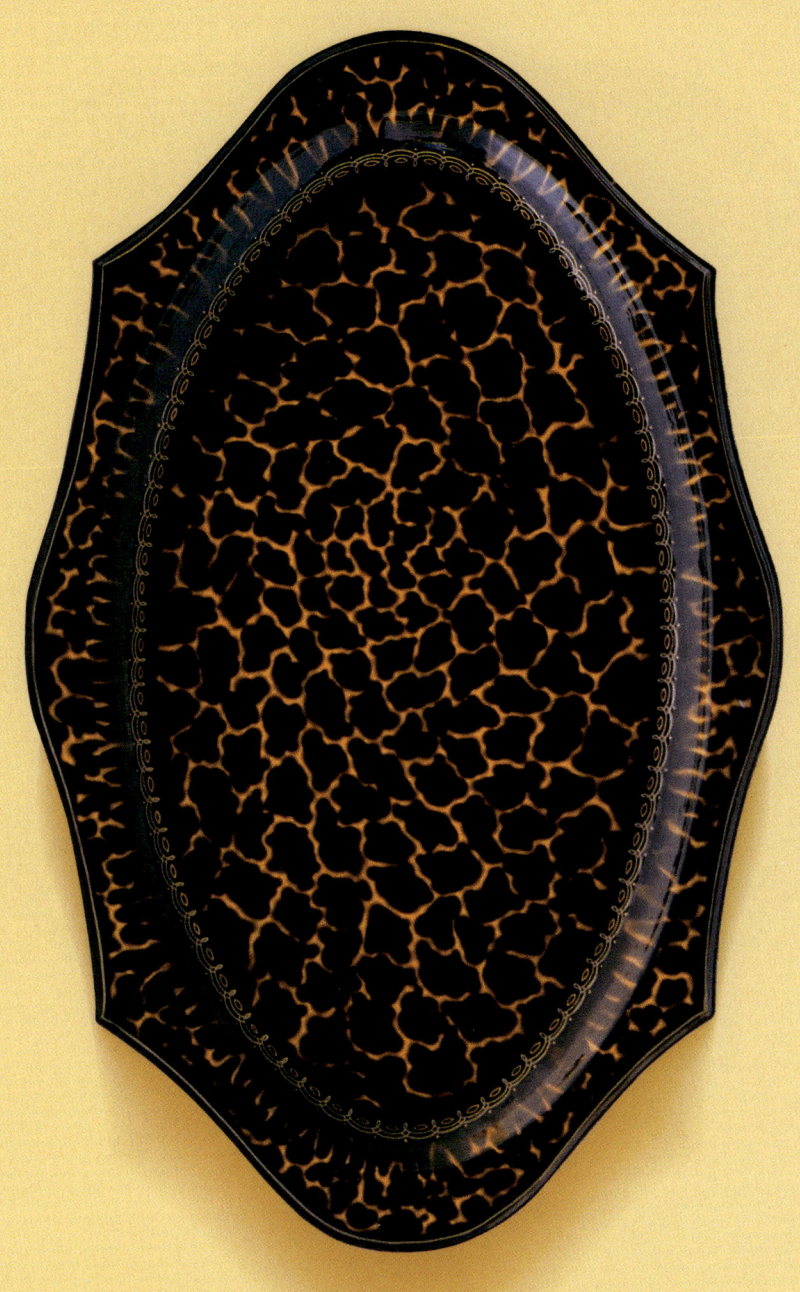

N.N. Antipov
"GALAXY"

2

N.N. Antipov
"EVENING WALTZ"

3

N.P. Antipov

4

N.P. Antipov

5

N.P. Antipov
"RUS"

6.

N.P. Antipov
"STILL LIFE"
7 — 8

A.I. Antipova
"FIGURED"

9

M.P. Antipova
"PETERSBURG"

10

G.P. Belyayev
"AUTUMN"

11

L.A. Belyayeva
"FIELD FLOWERS"

12

O.Y. Burbyshev

13

A.Y. Vishnyakov

14

L.N. Vishnyakov
"BUNCH OF FLOWERS"

15.

R.A. Vishnyakova
"ORNAMENTAL"

16.

R.A. Vishnyakova
"FLOWERS ON GREEN"
17 — 18

A.P. Gogin

19

A.P. Gogin

20

A.P. Gogin
"FLOWERS AND A BIRD"
21 — 23

N.I. Gogin

24

S.A. Golubkov
"BUNCH OF FLOWERS"
25

N.N. Goncharova
"FESTIVE"
26

N.N. Goncharova
"RESPLENDENT"

27

N.N. Goncharova
"TENDERNESS"

28

N.N. Goncharova
"JOY"
29

N.N. Goncharova
"FANTASIA"

30 — 32

N.N. Goncharova
"MELODY"

33

B.V. Grafov

34

B.V. Grafov
"A MORNING OUTSIDE
MOSCOW"

35

B.V. Grafov
"MORNING BOUQUET"

36

B.V. Grafov
"BUNCH OF FLOWERS"

37

B.V. Grafov
"DANDELION - TWINS"

38

B.V. Grafov
"GARDEN FLOWERS"
39

K.V. Gribkov

40

K.V. Gribkov

41

K.V. Gribkov
"BASKET WITH FLOWERS"

42

M.E. Domnikova
"EARTH'S GRAVITATION"

43

V.I. Dyuzhayev

44

V.I. Dyuzhayev

45

V.I. Dyuzhayev

46

V.I. Dyuzhayev

47

L.Y. Dyatlova
"SEPTEMBER"
48

L.Y. Dyatlova
*"BOUQUET AGAINST A WHITE
BACKGROUND"*

49

V.V. Zhmylev
"BOUQUET FROM AN ANGLE"

50

V.V. Kledov

51

V.V. Kledov
"FRESHNESS"

52

V.V. Kledov
"FRUITS"

53

N.S. Kledov
"BOUQUET AND FRUIT"

54

N.S. Kledov

55

N.S. Kledov

56

Z.A. Kledova
"RAINBOW"

57

P.S. Kurzin
"TOBACCO LEAVES"

58

P.S. Kurzin

59

Y.P. Lapshin

60

Y.P. Lapshin
"JUBILEE"

61

Y.P. Lapshin
"ROSES"

62

M.V. Lebedev
"RUSSIAN MOTIF"

63

A.I. Leznov
"BASKET WITH FRUIT"

64

A.I. Leznov
"FLOWERS"
65

A.I. Leznov
**"FLOWERS IN A BASKET
AND A BIRD"**

66

I.S. Leontiev

67

I.S. Leontiev

68

I.S. Leontiev

69

V.I. Letkov
"JOY"

70

A.N. Mazhayev
"ROSES"

71

N.N. Mazhayev

72

N.N. Mazhayev
"TWINKLE"

73 — 75

N.N. Mazhayev

76

N.N. Mazhayev
"SUMMER"

77

N.N. Mazhayev
"FRUIT"

78—80

N.N. Mazhayev
"MOSCOW ENVIRONS"

81

S.A. Filippov
"WREATH"

82

ПЕТРЪ

ВИШН

СЪ СЫН

Московскаго Уѣзда 2го С

Board XIX c.

Studio of T.M. Belyayev in
Zhostovo(?)
"PETER THE GREAT ON LAKE
LADOGA"

83

Studio of V.T. Belyayev
in Zhostovo (?)
S.A. Mitrofanov

84

Studio of O.F. Vishnyakov and sons
Peter and Vassily in Ostashkovo

85

Studio of O.F. Vishnyakov and sons
Peter and Vassily in Ostashkovo

86

Studio of O.F. Vishnyakov and sons
Peter and Vassily in Ostashkovo

87

Studio of O.F. Vishnyakov and sons
Peter and Vassily in Ostashkovo

88

Studio of O.F. Vishnyakov and sons
Peter and Vassily in Ostashkovo

89 — 90

*Studio of V.O. Vishnyakov in
Ostashkovo*

91

*Studio of V.O. Vishnyakov in
Ostashkovo*

92

*Studio of Y.F. and L.F. Vishnyakov
in Zhostovo*

93

Studio in vil. Novosiltsevo

94

M.R. Mitrofanov

95 — 96

M.R. Mitrofanov

97

N.A. Pichugina
**"WREATH OF FLOWERS
(FIELD)"**

98

N.A. Pichugina
"GARDEN FLOWERS"
99 — 101

P.I. Plakhov
**"FLOWERS, A BIRD
AND A BUTTERFLY"**

102

P.I. Plakhov
103

V.N. Pyzhov
"AUTUMN FLOWERS"

104—106

V.V. Rizin

107

B.A. Savelyev
"OLD MOTIF"
108

B.A. Savelyev
"TWO BRANCHES"

109

M.P. Savelyev
110

M.P. Savelyev
"RAIN"

111

M.P. Savelyev
"ELEGY"

112

M.P. Savelyev
"HORIZON"

113

M.P. Savelyev
"STILL LIFE WITH FRUIT"

114

T.N. Sholokhova
"OLD MOTIF"

115

T.N. Sholokhova
"EVENING GARDEN"

116

Catalogue
Bibliography

Catalogue compiled by
N.O. Krestovskaya

Catalogue

Antipov
Nikolai Nikolayevich
(b. 1960)
1. *"Jubilee"* decorative tray, 1990
Metal, oil, lacquer, smoking, decorative painting
54x68x2
Below: "Zhostovo Antipov N.N. 1990."
Russian Museum (RM), inventory No P-4925. Received from Russia's Culture Ministry in 1991.
2. *"Galaxy"* decorative tray, 1990
Metal, oil, lacquer, smoking, decorative painting
41x67x2.5
Below: "Antipov 1990 Zhostovo."
RM, inventory No P-4924. Received from Russia's Culture Ministry in 1991.
3. *"Evening Waltz"* tray, 1992
Metal, oil, lacquer, decorative painting
64x78x1.5
Author's property

Antipov
Nikolai Petrovich
(b. 1931),
Merited Artist of Russia
4. Tray, 1957
Metal, oil, lacquer, decorative painting
42.5x52.5x1.7
RM, inventory No P-2119. Received as a gift from the Metallopodnos artel in 1959.
5. Tray, 1972
Metal, oil, mother-of-pearl, metal powder, bronze, lacquer, decorative painting
Diameter 46x2
Below: "ANP," "Antipov N.P. 1972"
RM, inventory No P-3634. Received from the author in 1972.
6. *"Rus"* tray, 1976
Metal, oil, lacquer, decorative painting
54.5x77.5x1.5
Below: "Antipov N.P. 1976"
RM, inventory No P-4070. Received from Russia's Culture Ministry in 1979.

7 — 8 *"Still Life"* tray, 1993
Metal, oil, lacquer, decorative painting

Diameter 70x2.5

Antipova
Anna Ilyinichna
(b. 1927)
9. *"Figured"* tray, 1992
Metal, oil, lacquer, mother-of-pearl, decorative painting
Diameter 70x2.5

Antipova
Marina Petrovna
(b. 1963)
10. *"Petersburg"* tray, 1993
Metal, oil, lacquer, decorative painting
62x76x2.5
Author's property

Belyayev
Gennady Petrovich
(b. 1938)
11. *"Autumn"* tray, 1975
Metal, oil, mother-of-pearl, Dutch gold, bronze, lacquer, decorative painting
45.5x58.5x2.3
Museum of Folk Art (MFA), inventory No КП-20436. Received from the Zhostovo Painted Tray Factory in 1976.

Belyayeva
Lidia Alexandrovna
(b. 1935)
12. *"Field Flowers"* tray, 1993
Metal, oil, lacquer, decorative painting
47x60x1.8

Burbyshev
Osip Yefimovich
(1867-1919)
13. Tray, 1890s
Metal, oil, metal powder, lacquer, decorative painting
46.5x61.5x3.1
RM, inventory No P-3671. Received from R. I. Blagova of Zhostovo in 1974.

Vishnyakov
Alexander
(Afanasy) Yegorovich
(ca. 1855 - late 1930s)
14. Tray, 1920s
Metal, oil, bronze, lacquer, decorative painting

33.5x42.5x1.5
MFA, inventory No MXП-2609. Purchased in 1925.

Vishnyakov
Lev Nikolayevich
(1931-1985)
15. *"Bunch of Flowers"* tray, 1983
Metal, oil, lacquer, decorative painting
47x60x1.8

Vishnyakova
Rufima Alexeyevna
(b. 1935)
16. *"Ornamental"* tray, 1992
Metal, oil, lacquer, decorative painting
53x67x1.8

17 — 18. *"Flowers on Green"* tray, 1993
Metal, oil, lacquer, decorative painting
44x58x1.8

Gogin
Andrei Pavlovich
(1893-1980), Merited Figure of Arts
of the Russian Federation, winner
of the Repin State Prize
19. Tray, 1963
Metal, oil, bronze, lacquer, decorative painting
81x97.5x2.5
RM, inventory No P-3018. Purchased through Moscow's Handicrafts Store in 1969.
20. Tray, 1975
Metal, oil, bronze, lacquer, decorative painting
58x74x1.8
Bottom right: "Gogin А.П."
RM, inventory No P-4026. Received from the author in 1975.

21 — 23. *"Flowers and a Bird",* 1951
Metal, oil, lacquer, decorative painting
80x63x2.5
MFA

Gogin
Nikolai Ivanovich
(b. 1931)
24. Tray, 1957
Metal, oil, lacquer, decorative painting
42.7x52.5x1.5
Below: "Gogin H. 1957"

RM, inventory No P-2120. Received as a gift from the Metallopodnos Artel in 1959.

Golubkov
Sergei Alexeyevich
(b. 1961)

25. *"Bunch of Flowers"* tray, 1990
Metal, oil, lacquer, decorative painting
47x67x2
Below: "Golubkov C.A."
RM, inventory No P-4962. Received from Russia's Culture Ministry in 1991.

Goncharova
Nina Nikolayevna
(b. 1927), Merited Artist of Russia, winner of the Repin State Prize

26. *"Festive"* tray, 1978
Metal, oil, metal power, lacquer, decorative painting
64.5x79x2.5
Below: "Goncharova H.H."
RM, inventory No P-4250. Received from Russia's Culture Ministry in 1979.

27. *"Resplendent"* tray, 1989
Metal, oil, mother-of-pearl, Dutch gold, lacquer, decorative painting
47x60x1.5
Below: "Goncharova H.H. 1989. Zhostovo"
RM, inventory No P-4922. Received from Russia's Culture Ministry in 1991.

28. *"Tenderness"* tray, 1985
Metal, oil, lacquer, decorative painting
60x75x1.5
In the center: "Goncharova H.H. 1985."
RM, inventory No P-4679. Received from Russia's Culture Ministry in 1988.

29. *"Joy"* tray, 1986
Metal, oil, Dutch gold, bronze, lacquer, decorative painting
52.5x64.5x2
Below: "Goncharova H.H."
RM, inventory No P-4886. Received from Russia's Culture Ministry in 1988.

30 — 32. *"Fantasia"* tray, 1991
Metal, oil, bronze, lacquer, decorative painting
64x80x2.5
Author's property

33. *"Melody"* tray, 1992
Metal, oil, lacquer, mother-of-pearl, decorative painting
45x58x1.8

Grafov
Boris Vasilyevich
(b. 1933), Merited Artist of Russia

34. Decorative tray, 1976
Metal, oil, bronze, lacquer, decorative painting
48x48x1.8
Below: "B.G.," "1976"
RM, inventory No P-4037. Received from the author in 1977.

35. *"A Morning Outside Moscow"* tray, 1978
Metal, oil, lacquer, decorative painting
59x80x2.5
Bottom left: "B. Grafov. 1978"
RM, inventory No P-4252. Received from Russia's Culture Ministry in 1979.

36. *"Morning Bouquet"* tray, 1980
Metal, oil, metal powder, lacquer, decorative painting
46.5x60x3
Below: "B. Grafov"
RM, inventory No P-4323. Received from the author in 1980.

37. *"Bunch of Flowers"* tray, 1990
Metal, oil, lacquer, decorative painting
53x67x2

38. *"Dandelion - Twins"* decorative tray, 1990
Metal, oil, gold powder, lacquer, decorative painting
Diameter 50x2
Below: "B. Grafov." "Twins"
RM, inventory No P-4923. Received from Russia's Culture Ministry in 1991.

39. *"Garden Flowers"* tray, 1993
Metal, oil, lacquer, decorative painting
64x78x2.5

Gribkov
Konstantin Vasilyevich
(ca.1860-1926)

40. Tray, 1920s
Metal, oil, bronze, lacquer, decorative painting
Diameter 32x3
MFA, inventory No MXП-2580. Received in 1926.

41. Tray (after A. Suvorov's drawing), 1920s
Metal, oil, bronze, lacquer, decorative painting
36.5x36.5x1.7
MFA, inventory No MXП-2524

42. *"Basket with Flowers"* tray, 1920s
Metal, oil, bronze, lacquer, decorative

painting
53x68.5x2
Zhostovo Factory Fund (ZFF). Received from K. V. Yashkova of Zhostovo in 1950

Domnikova
Marina Efimovna
(b. 1959)

43. *"Earth's Gravitation"* tray, 1987
Metal, oil, lacquer, decorative painting
64.5x77.8x2
Below: "Domnikova"
RM, inventory No P-4888. Received from Russia's Culture Ministry in 1990.

Dyuzhayev
Vassily Ilyich
(1913-1987)

44. Tray, 1955
Metal, oil, metal powder, lacquer, decorative painting
42x56.5x1.5
MFA, inventory No КП-5302. Received from the Zhostovo Painted Tray Factory in 1956.

45. Tray, 1977
Metal, oil, lacquer, decorative painting
63.5x78.5x2.2
Below: "V. Dyuzhayev 26/5/77"
RM, inventory No P-4297. Received from the author in 1980.

46. Tray, 1979
Metal, oil, lacquer, decorative painting
45.5x69.5x2
Below: "V. Dyuzhayev 28/7/79"
RM, inventory No P-4296. Received from the author in 1980.

47. Tray, 1979
Metal, oil, lacquer, decorative painting
44x34.5x1.6
Below: "V. Dyuzhayev 1979"
RM, inventory No P-4298. Received from the author in 1980.

Dyatlova
Larisa Yurievna
*(b. 1957),
winner of Prize from the Young Communist League Central Committee*

48. *"September"* tray, 1987
Metal, oil, bronze, lacquer, decorative painting
46.5x60x1.5
RM, inventory No P-4892. Received

from Russia's Culture Ministry in 1990.

49. *"Bouquet Against a White Background"* tray, 1992
Metal, oil, lacquer, decorative painting
45x56x2.5
Author's property

Zhmylev
Vladimir Vasilyevich
(b. 1935),
winner of the Repin State Prize

50. *"Bouquet from an Angle"* tray, 1989
Metal, oil, lacquer, decorative painting
53x67x2.5

Kledov
Victor Vasilyevich
(b. 1933),
Merited Artist of Russia

51. Tray, 1977
Metal, oil, lacquer, decorative painting
56.5x60.5x1.5
Below: "8.77. Kledov V.V."
RM, inventory No P-4104. Received from Russia's Culture Ministry in 1978.

52. *"Freshness"* tray, 1990
Metal, oil, lacquer, decorative painting
62x78x2
Below: "Kledov V.V."
RM, inventory No P-4915. Received from Russia's Culture Ministry in 1991.

53. *"Fruits"* tray, 1992
Metal, oil, lacquer, decorative painting
53x67x1.8

Kledov
Nikita Stepanovich
(1879-1947)

54. *"Bouquet and Fruit"* tray, 1930s
Metal, oil, metal powder, lacquer, decorative painting
51x66x3
ZFF. Received from the author's family in 1948.

55. Tray, 1930s
Metal, oil, bronze, lacquer, decorative painting
41x51x1.7
ZFF. Received from fellow-villagers in 1949.

56. Tray, 1930s
Metal, oil, bronze, lacquer, decorative painting
41x51x1.7
ZFF. Received from the author's family

in 1948.

Kledova
Zoya Alexandrovna
(b. 1924),
Merited Artist of Russia

57. *"Rainbow"* tray, 1971
Metal, oil, bronze, lacquer, decorative painting
Diameter 70.2x1.6
Below: "Z. Kledova"
RM, inventory No P-3631. Received from the author in 1971.

Kurzin
Pavel Stepanovich
(ca. 1884-1939)

58. *"Tobacco Leaves"* tray, 1920s
Metal, oil, metal powder, bronze, lacquer, decorative painting
32.5x42.5x1.6
ZFF. Received from fellow-villagers in 1946.

59. Tray, 1930s
Metal, oil, metal powder, smoking, lacquer, decorative painting
41.5x52.5x2.2
RM, inventory No P-3670. Received from R.A. Vishnyakova of Zhostovo in 1974.

Lapshin
Yevgeny Petrovich
(b. 1933),
Merited Artist of Russia,
winner of the Repin State Prize

60. Tray, 1971
Metal, oil, metal powder, lacquer, decorative painting
57x68x1.5
Below: "Lapshin Y. 1971"
RM, inventory No P-3632. Received from the author in 1971.

61. *"Jubilee"* tray, 1976
Metal, oil, lacquer, decorative painting
64x78x2
Left edge: "Y. Lapshin 1976"
RM, inventory No P-4018. Received from the author in 1977.

62. *"Roses"* tray, 1993

Lebedev
Mikhail Viktorovich
(b. 1962)

63. *"Russian Motif"* tray, 1992

Metal, oil, lacquer, mother-of-pearl, decorative painting
48x65x2.5

Leznov
Alexei Ilyich
(1886-1946)

64. *"Basket with Fruit"* tray, 1930
Metal, oil, bronze, lacquer, decorative painting
Diameter 67x2.5
Below: "Paint. Leznov A. 14/6/30 SHKU"
MFA, inventory No MXП-2531. Received from the Handicrafts School (ShKU) of the village of Troitskoye in 1930.

65. *"Flowers"* tray, 1930
Metal, oil, bronze, lacquer, decorative painting
Diameter 68x2.5
Below: "Paint. Leznov A. 6/30 SHKU"
MFA, inventory No MXП-2591. Received from the Handicrafts School (ShKU) of the village of Troitskoye in 1930.

66. *"Flowers in a Basket and a Bird"* tray, 1930
Metal, oil, bronze, lacquer, decorative painting
Diameter 68x2.5
Below: "Leznov A. 6/2/30 SHKU"
MFA, inventory No MXП-2590. Received from the Handicrafts School (ShKU) of the village of Troitskoye in 1930.

Leontiev
Ivan Stepanovich
(1875-1945)

67. Tray, 1920s
Metal, oil, bronze, lacquer, decorative painting
42x56.5x2
ZFF. Received from N.I. Belyayev of Zhostovo in 1974.

68. Tray, 1937
Metal, oil, metal powder, bronze, lacquer, decorative painting
40x40x2.5
MFA, inventory No MXП-2570. Intended for the Paris World Fair; received in 1937.

69. Tray, 1937
Metal, oil, metal powder, lacquer, dec-

orative painting
43x58x2
MFA, inventory No MXII-2567. Intended for the Paris World Fair; received in 1937.

Letkov
Viacheslav Ivanovich
(b. 1939),
Merited Artist of Russia, winner of the Repin State Prize
70. *"Joy"* tray, 1992
Metal, oil, lacquer, decorative painting
64x78x2.5

Mazhayev
Alexander Nikolayevich
(b. 1937)
71. *"Roses"* tray, 1963
Metal, oil, lacquer, decorative painting
47x60x1.5

Mazhayev
Nikolai Nikolayevich
(b. 1937),
winner of the Repin State Prize,
Merited Artist of Russia
72. Tray, 1971
Metal, oil, lacquer, decorative painting
53x67x1.6
RM, inventory No P-3630. Received from the author in 1971.
73 — 75. *"Twinkle"* tray, 1993
Metal, oil, lacquer, mother-of-pearl, decorative painting
62x80x2.5
76. Tray, 1976
Metal, oil, lacquer, decorative painting
63x77x1.8
Below: "Mazhayev"
RM, inventory No P-4019. Received from the author in 1977.
77. *"Summer"* tray, 1980
Metal, oil, lacquer, decorative painting
63x76x2
Below: "Mazhayev"
RM, inventory No P-4324. Received from the author in 1982.
78 — 80. *"Fruit"* tray, 1993
Metal, oil, lacquer, decorative painting
47x60x2
81. *"Moscow Environs"* tray, 1990
Metal, oil, metal powder, lacquer, decorative painting

54x72x2
Below: "Mazhayev"
RM, inventory No P-B/X. Received from Russia's Culture Ministry 1991.

Filippov
Sergei Anatolyevich
(b. 1959)
82. *"Wreath"* tray, 1988
Metal, oil, metal powder, Dutch gold, lacquer, decorative painting
67x80.5x1.5
RM, inventory No P-4890. Received from Russia's Culture Ministry in 1990.

Studio
of Timofei Maximovich Belyayev in Zhostovo(?)
from 1830
83. *"Peter the Great on Lake Ladoga"* tray
Mid-19th cent.
Metal, oil, Dutch gold, lacquer, decorative painting
Painted after a lithograph from the French artist C. Steiben's Peter the Great in a Storm on Lake Ladoga," 1812
53.5x70.5x3
On the reverse a seal with encircled letters "F.T.B."
RM, inventory No P-4592. Received from T.D. Golovina of Gatchina in 1986.

Studio
of Vasiliy Timofeevich Belyayev in Zhostovo (?)

Mitrofanov
S.A.
(ca. 1850-1934)
84. Tray, late 19th cent.
Metal, oil, lacquer, decorative painting
50x69x2
RM, inventory No P-1555. Received from the Handicrafts Museum (St. Petersburg - Leningrad)

Studio
of Osip Filippovich Vishnyakov and sons Peter and Vassily in Ostashkovo
1825-1888
85. Tray, 1870s
Metal, oil, metal powder, lacquer, decorative painting

54x69x2.5
The reverse bears the trademark with three medals under the crown - the Fifth Moscow Exhibition of Russian Manufactures of 1865 with the profile of Alexander II; the Moscow Polytechnic Exhibition of 1872 with the double-headed eagle; the All-Russia Manufacture Exhibition in St. Petersburg of 1870 with the profile of Alexander II; below a band "to VISHNYAKOV AND SONS"
RM, inventory No P-3793. Received from M.P. Kazachkov of Leningrad in 1974
86. Tray, 1880s
Metal, oil, metal powder, gold and silver foil, lacquer, decorative painting
46.5x60x2
The reverse bears the trademark with three medals under the crown - the All-Russia Art and Industry Exhibition of 1882 with the profile of Alexander III; the Moscow Polytechnic Exhibition of 1872 with the double-headed eagle; the Fifth Moscow Exhibition of Russian Manufactures of 1865 with the profile of Alexander II; below a band "to VISHNYAKOV AND SONS" and an inscription "MOSCOW UYEZD 2nd DISTRICT VIL. OSTASHKOVO"
RM, inventory No P-3614. Received from N.N. Yakovlev of Leningrad in 1971.
87. Tray, 1880s
Metal, oil, Dutch gold, lacquer, decorative painting
46.5x61x2.3
The reverse bears the trademark with three medals under the crown - the All-Russia Art and Industry Exhibition of 1882 with the profile of Alexander III; the Moscow Polytechnic Exhibition of 1872 with the double-headed eagle; the Fifth Moscow Exhibition of Russian Manufactures of 1865 with the profile of Alexander II; below a band "to VISHNYAKOV AND SONS"
RM, inventory No P-3792. Received from M.P. Kazachkov of Leningrad in 1974.

88. Tray, 1880s
Metal, oil, metal powder, lacquer, decorative painting
46.5x60.5x2.5
The reverse bears the trademark with three medals under the crown - the All-Russia Art and Industry Exhibition of 1882 with the profile of Alexander III;

the Moscow Polytechnic Exhibition of 1872 with the double-headed eagle; the Fifth Moscow Exhibition of Russian Manufactures of 1865 with the profile of Alexander II; below a band "to VISHNYAKOV AND SONS" and an inscription "MOSCOW UYEZD 2nd DISTRICT VIL. OSTASHKOVO"
RM, inventory No P-4475. Received from Lenkomissiontorg in 1985.

89 — 90. Tray, 1880s
Metal, oil, lacquer, decorative painting
46.5x59.5x2.5
The reverse bears the trademark with three medals under the crown - the All-Russia Art and Industry Exhibition of 1882 with the profile of Alexander III; the Moscow Polytechnic Exhibition of 1872 with the double-headed eagle; the Fifth Moscow Exhibition of Russian Manufactures of 1865 with the profile of Alexander II; below a band "to VISHNYAKOV AND SONS" and an inscription "MOSCOW UYEZD 2nd DISTRICT VIL. OSTASHKOVO"
RM, inventory No P-3794. Received from M.P. Kazachkov of Leningrad in 1974.

Studio
of Vassily Osipovich Vishnyakov in Ostashkovo
1877-1916

91. Tray, late 1880s
Metal, oil, metal powder, lacquer, decorative painting
30.5x38.5x2.2
The reverse bears the trademark with an inscription "to V. O. VISHNYAKOV" above the representation of the two sides of medals - the All-Russia Art and Industry Exhibition of 1882 in Moscow and the Moscow Handicrafts Exhibition of 1885.
RM, inventory No P-1563. Received from the Handicrafts Museum (St. Petersburg-Leningrad) in 1938.

92. Tray, 1880-1890s
Metal, oil, metal powder, lacquer, decorative painting
47.5x61x2
The reverse bears the trademark with the representation of the two sides of medals - the Moscow Handicrafts Exhibition of 1885; the All-Russia Art and Industry Exhibition of 1882 in Moscow; the All-Russia Agricultural Exhibition of

1887 in Kharkov; below an inscription "to V. O. VISHNYAKOV."
RM, inventory No P-3672. Received from Y. P. Lapshin of Zhostovo in 1974.

Studio
of Yegor Filippovich and Leonty Filippovich Vishnyakov in Zhostovo
1880-1890s

93. Tray, 1880-1890s
Metal, oil, lacquer, decorative painting
31.2x41.5x2
The reverse bears the trademark "Brothers Y.F. L.F. Vishnyakovs."
RM, inventory No P-1564. Received from the Handicrafts Museum (St. Petersburg-Leningrad) in 1938.

Studio
in vil. Novosiltsevo

94. Tray, early 20th cent.
Metal, oil, bronze, smoking, lacquer, decorative painting
51x38.5x2.2
MFA, inventory No MXП-2522. Received from the Novosiltsevo Handicrafts School.

Mitrofanov
Matvei Rodionovich
(1889-1975)

95 — 96. Tray, 1950s
Metal, oil, metal powder, bronze, lacquer, decorative painting
52.5x66.5x1.7
ZFF. Received from the author in the 1950s.

97. Tray, 1955
Metal, oil, metal powder, bronze, lacquer, decorative painting
53x66.5x1.9
ZFF. Received from the author in 1957.

Pichugina
Nadezhda Alexandrovna
(b. 1935)

98. "Wreath of Flowers (Field)" tray, 1991
Metal, oil, lacquer, decorative painting
61x74x2
RM, inventory No P-4884. Received from Russia's Culture Ministry in 1990.

99 — 101. "Garden Flowers" tray, 1991
Metal, oil, lacquer, decorative painting
62x80x2.5

Plakhov
Pavel Ivanovich
(b. 1915)

102. "Flowers, a Bird and a Butterfly" tray, 1950
Metal, oil, metal powder, lacquer, decorative painting
45.5x61x1.7
ZFF. Received from the author in the 1950s.

103. Tray, 1957
Metal, oil, bronze, lacquer, decorative painting
51.5x65.5x1.5
ZFF. Received from the author in 1957.

Pyzhov
Vladimir Nikolayevich
(b. 1945)

104—106. "Autumn Flowers" tray, 1985
Metal, oil, bronze, gold leaf, lacquer, decorative painting
67x81x2
Below: "Pyzhov V.N. Zhostovo 1985"
RM, inventory No P-4676. Received from Russia's Culture Ministry in 1988.

Rizin
Vassily Vassiliyevich
(b. 1959)

107. Tray, 1987
Metal, oil, lacquer, decorative painting
62x78x2.5
Bottom right: "Rizin V. 1987"
RM, inventory No P-4645. Received from the author in 1987.

Savelyev
Boris Andreyevich
(b. 1949)

108. "Old Motif" tray, 1985
Metal, oil, lacquer, decorative painting
56x71x2
Bottom right: "Savelyev B. 1985"
RM, inventory No P-4598. Received from the author in 1987.

109. *"Two Branches"* tray, 1986
Metal, oil, lacquer, hand forging, decorative painting
60.5x80x2
Bottom left: "Savelyev B.A. 1986"
RM, inventory No P-4599. Received from the author in 1987.

Savelyev
Mikhail Petrovich
(b. 1930),
Merited Artist of Russia,
winner of the Repin State Prize
110. Tray, 1971
Metal, oil, metal powder, lacquer, decorative painting
Diameter 67.5x1.5

Below: "Savelyev Zhostovo 29/11/71"
RM, inventory No H-3627. Received from the author in 1971.
111. *"Rain"* tray, 1977
Metal, oil, lacquer, decorative painting
61x76.5x2
Below: "M. Savelyev 1977"
RM, inventory No P-4106. Received from Russia's Culture Ministry in 1978.
112. *"Elegy"* decorative tray, 1988
Metal, oil, metal powder, lacquer, decorative painting
Diameter 70x1.5
RM, inventory No P-4891. Received from Russia's Culture Ministry in 1990.
113. *"Horizon"* panel, 1980
Metal, oil, lacquer, decorative painting
Diameter 50x1.8

Below: "M. Savelyev 1980"
RM, inventory No P-4322. Received from the author in 1980.
114. *"Still Life with Fruit"* tray, 1993
Metal, oil, lacquer, decorative painting
64x78x2.5

Sholokhova
Tatyana Nikolayevna
(b. 1967)
115. *"Old Motif"* tray, 1992
Metal, oil, lacquer, mother-of-pearl, decorative painting
64x82x2.5
116. *"Evening Garden"* tray, 1993
Metal, oil, lacquer, mother-of-pearl, decorative painting, 66x72

Bibliography

Бакушинский А.В. Русские художественные лаки//Искусство. 1933. № 6.

Бакушинский А.В. Федоскино и Жостово (лаки)/В кн.: Народное искусство в художественных промыслах. Т. 1. — М.—Л., 1940.

Богуславская И.Я., Графов Б.В. Искусство Жостова. — Л., 1979.

Богуславская И.Я. Цветы Жостова/В кн.: Добрых рук мастерство. — Л., 1981.

Боруцкий В. Кустарное производство лакированных вещей из папье-маше/В кн.: Кустарная промышленность России. Разные промыслы. Т. 2. — СПб, 1913.

Василенко В.М. Выставка русских художественных лаков//Промысловая кооперация. 1933. № 3.

Графов Б.В. Задачи художников Жостова/В кн.: Творческие проблемы современных народных художественных промыслов. — Л., 1981.

Дьяков Л.А. Проблема художественного качества в искусстве Федоскина и Жостова/В сб.: Проблемы народного искусства. — М., 1982.

Дьяков Л.А. Связь поколений в творчестве жостовского мастера А.П. Гогина/В кн.: Народные мастера. Традиции, школы. — М., 1985.

Жостовский расписной поднос/Каталог выставки. — М., 1976.

Исаев А.А. Промыслы Московской губернии. Т. 2. — М., 1876.

Искусство Жостова. Современные мастера/Сост. И.А. Романова. — М., 1987.

Коромыслов Б.И. Борис Графов/В кн.: Советское декоративное искусство. Вып. 7. — М., 1983.

Коромыслов Б.И. Букет цветов. — М., 1962.

Коромыслов Б.И. Жостовская роспись. — М., 1977.

Коромыслов Б.И. О творческой основе исполнительского мастерства в искусстве жостовской роспи-
си/Сб. трудов НИИХП. Вып. 7. — М., 1973.

Коромыслов Б.И. Проблемы развития жостовского искусства/В кн.: Искусство художественных промыслов на современном этапе. Сб. трудов НИИХП. — М., 1982.

Коромыслов Б.И. Современное искусство Жостова. Высказывания художников о своем творчестве/Сб. трудов НИИХП. Вып. 9. — М., 1979.

Крапивина И.А. А.И. Лёзнов. — М., 1961.

Крапивина И.А. Из истории жостовского промысла (XIX—нач. XX в.)/В кн.: Русский город (исследования и материалы). Вып. 5. — М., 1982.

Крапивина И.А. Жостовскому промыслу 150 лет.//Декоративное искусство. 1975. № 9.

Крапивина И.А. О работе института с Жостовским промыслом/Сб. трудов НИИХП. Вып. 3. — М., 1966.

Крапивина И.А. Роспись по металлу/В кн.: Русское декоративное искусство. Т. 3. — М., 1965.

Масленников Н.Н., Бакушинский А.В Русские художественные лаки. — М., 1933.

Пискунова Л.С. Русские росписные лаковые железные изделия (опыт изучения коллекции историко-бытового отдела Гос. Русского музея)/В кн.: Записки историко-бытового отдела ГРМ. Вып. 2. — Л., 1932.

Промыслы Московской губернии/Сб. статистич. сведений по Московской губернии. Т. 7. Вып. 3. — М., 1882.

Рождественская С.Б. К вопросу о судьбах художественных промыслов РСФСР (подносный промысел Нижнего Тагила)//Советская этнография. 1960. № 2.

Романова И.А. Федоскино и Жостово. Выставка произведений современных мастеров миниатюрной живописи и декоративной росписи/Каталог. — М., 1984.

Русские художественные промыслы (вторая половина XIX—XX в.). — М., 1965.

Соловьева Л.Н. Эстетика жостовского подноса/В кн.: Искусство лаковой миниатюры и декоративной росписи по металлу. Сб. науч. трудов НИИХП. — М., 1990

Темерин С.М. Русское прикладное искусство. Советские годы. Очерки. — М., 1960.

Уханова И.Н. Русские лаки в собрании Эрмитажа. — Л., 1964.

Яловенко Г.В. Жостово/В кн.: Народное декоративное искусство РСФСР. — М., 1957.

Яловенко Г.В. Русские художественные лаки. — М., 1959.

Krapiwina I. Russische handbemalte Tabletts. — L., 1981.

Masterpieces of Russian Folk Art

Irina Ya. Boguslavskaya

ZHOSTOVO *album*
Painted Trays

Director	*Gennady Popov*
Managing director	*Irina Sitnikova*
Editor	*Tatiana Ryutina*
Computer comp.	*Sergei Shilko*
Computer lay-out	*Tatiana Anosova*
Corrector	*Elena Dubchenko*

Bl. 5, 7/10, Starosadsky pereulok, 101000, Moscow, Russia
Phone: (095) 921 39 52, fax: (095) 921 39 20
Printed by Interbook